Introduction

Bob Griese is the calm, fast-thinking quarterback for the Miami Dolphins football team.

He had talent, but Bob had to work hard to become the great quarterback that he is today.

It is largely due to Bob Griese that the Dolphins have climbed from being a last-place team to one of the strongest teams in pro football.

Bob Griese

S. H. Burchard

Illustrated with photographs
and with drawings by Paul Frame

Harcourt Brace Jovanovich
New York and London

PHOTO CREDITS
Purdue University, photograph by David Umberger,
    pp. 16, 18.
United Press International, cover, pp. 2, 20, 21, 22, 23, 25,
    27, 29, 30, 35, 36, 38, 40, 43, 45, 46, 48, 50–51, 53, 55, 56,
    58–59, 60, 62.

Frontispiece: Bob Griese calling signals

Printed in the United States of America

First edition

B C D E F G H I J K

Library of Congress Cataloging in Publication Data

Burchard, S   H
    Sports star, Bob Griese.

    SUMMARY: An easy-to-read biography of the quarter-
back who led the Miami Dolphins from being a last place
team to one of the strongest teams in pro football.
    1. Griese, Bob—Juvenile literature. 2. Foot-
ball—Juvenile literature. [1. Griese, Bob. 2. Football—Biography] I. Title.
GV939.G76B87   796.33′2′0924 [B] [92]   75-11779
ISBN 0-15-277997-3
ISBN 0-15-684820-1 (pbk)

Contents

1

Growing Up in Evansville

"Look, Mom!" said young Bob
    Griese.
"I can juggle three eggs at
    once!"
"Be careful!" warned his
    mother.
Splat! The eggs broke all over
    the kitchen floor.
When Bob Griese was a little
    boy, he loved to juggle
    things.

He juggled anything round, but
he soon gave up on eggs.
They were too messy.
Bob grew up in Evansville,
Indiana, with his older
brother named Bill and his
younger sister named Joyce.
His father owned a plumbing
business.
The Griese family had many
good times together.
When Bob was ten years old, a
terrible thing happened.
His father suddenly died.
Then life changed for the
Grieses.

The plumbing business was
   sold, and Mrs. Griese went
   to work as a secretary.
The family did not have such
   good times any more.
Bob became very quiet.
He missed his father.

When he and his sister and
brother were old enough,
they did odd jobs to earn
extra money.
Bob also grew to like sports.
He felt good when he played
ball.
In grade school he played
football, baseball, and
basketball.
When Bob was ready for the
ninth grade, he went to a
new school.
It was called Rex Mundi High.
Bob played on the school's first
football team.

None of the players knew
   much about the game.
Coach Coudret had to work
   hard.
He had to teach the boys what
   the rules were and how to
   play the game.

Bob learned that he had to
practice often in order to be
good.
The Rex Mundi football team
did not win many games
their first year, but they were
great in the next three years.
Bob Griese played quarterback.
He became the leader of the
team.
Bob was very smart.
He could tell what the other
team was going to do, and he
almost always called the
right plays.
But he was not a good passer.

He put his arm out to the side
  to throw.
He could not put a spin on his
  passes, and the ball did not
  go very far.

Still Bob was a speedy runner.
He also called the plays that
led to victory after victory.

Many colleges wanted Bob
    Griese on their team.
He decided to go to Purdue
    University.
He liked the coaches there,
    and Purdue had winning
    football teams.
Most of all, Bob thought
    he would get the kind of
    education he wanted at
    Purdue.
He needed money to take care
    of his family.
He wanted to learn how to
    become a businessman.

2

Purdue University Star

Bob played on the freshman
    team during his first year at
    Purdue.
He still had trouble passing.
His balls wobbled in the air,
    but he did everything else
    well.
He was a natural leader.
Coach Bob DeMoss wanted
    Griese to be the team
    quarterback.

17

He taught Bob how to throw
  better.
Bob was an able student and
  learned to throw overhand.
By his second year he had all
  the skills he needed.

He was the starting varsity
quarterback.
Bob was great in his first game.
He led two long drives and
scored two touchdowns.
He kicked the two extra points,
and he also got off a 36-yard
field goal.
In fact, Bob made all the points
in the game!
The final score was 17 to 0.
It was a great beginning.
Football fans everywhere
talked about the amazing
quarterback who could run,
pass, and kick.

A winter day at Purdue

These photos, taken one after another, show the kind of problems Bob Griese comes up against in college football.

Big No. 85 comes after Bob.

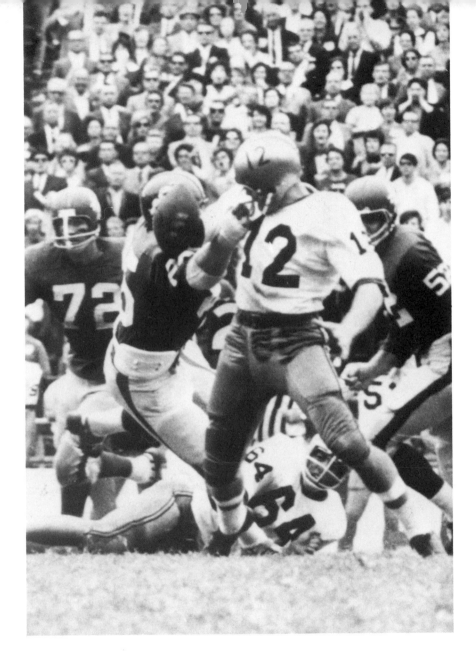

Bob tries to break away from his tacklers.

Griese gets past No. 85, but another huge tackler
(No. 52) closes in on him . . .

and drags him backward for a loss.

The next game was not so easy.
Purdue met the Fighting Irish
    of Notre Dame.
Bob tried to get past the Notre
    Dame line, but three of his
    passes were intercepted.
He lost yards when he ran
    back to throw the ball.
Purdue lost by a score of 35 to
    14.
It was Bob's first big-time loss.
He did not like losing.
The next year Bob was
    determined to beat Notre
    Dame.
It would not be easy.

Griese has trouble passing
during the Notre Dame game.

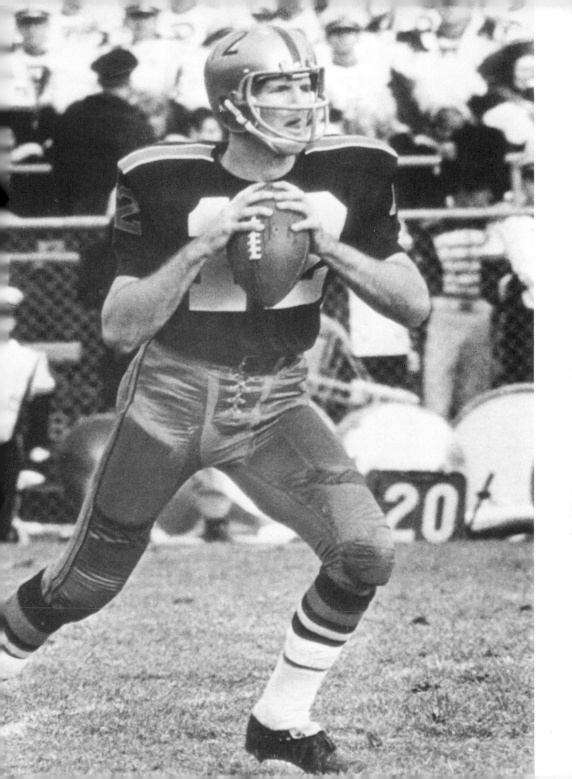

The Fighting Irish were rated
   the number one team in the
   nation.
Griese attacked through the air.
It was the only way to get by
   the huge Notre Dame line.
Bob did not miss.
Once he completed thirteen
   passes in a row.
But Notre Dame was good, too.
With one minute to go in the
   game, the Irish were ahead
   21 to 18.
Purdue had the ball.
The big Notre Dame tackles
   got ready to smash into Bob
   Griese before he could

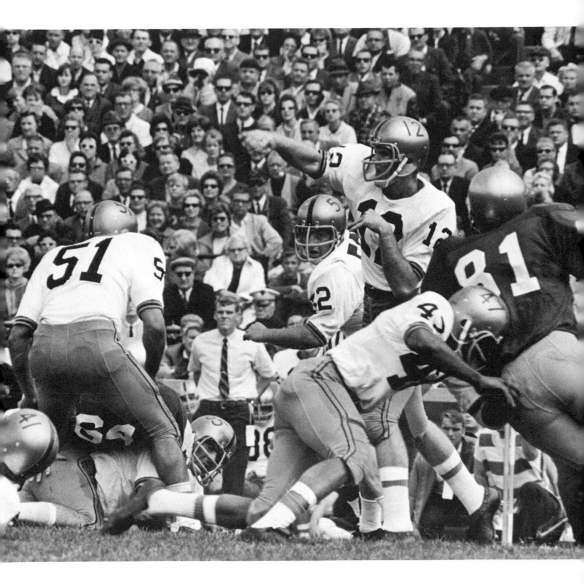

This time Bob is able to complete
his passes against Notre Dame.

get his arm up to pass.
Bob took four quick steps to
the side and hurled the ball.
A Purdue player caught it on
the Irish three-yard line.
With seconds to go, Bob calmly
handed the ball to his fullback, who pushed over the
goal line for the winning
touchdown.
It was one of the greatest
victories in the history of
Purdue football.
"Bob Griese put on the finest
show I have ever seen," said
the Notre Dame coach after
the game.

Purdue football champions, in California
for the Rose Bowl game,
meet the governor, Ronald Reagan.

3

Bob's First Pro Game

Bob Griese went on to become
one of the best college
quarterbacks in the country.
By his senior year he decided
to turn pro.
He was the first choice of a
new team called the Miami
Dolphins.
Bob liked the idea of playing
for a new team because he

Purdue super star Bob Griese

thought he would get to play
sooner.
But he did not expect to play
in the very first game of the
season.
The game was against the
Denver Broncos.
Big John Stofa was the starting
quarterback for the Dolphins.
Bob watched Stofa call three
plays.
On the fourth play there was a
pileup of bodies.
The players began getting up—
all but Big John.
Stofa lay on his back.
He was writhing in pain.

32

People gathered around him,
and someone called for a
stretcher.
After just four plays Stofa was
finished.
His ankle was broken.

Coach Wilson told Griese to
  warm up.
The crowd booed when Bob
  ran onto the field.
They had come to watch John
  Stofa lead the team.
But Bob played it cool.
He called the right plays.
In the second period he
  marched the team down the
  field for an 80-yard touch-
  down drive.
At half time the Dolphins led
  by a score of 14 to 0.
In the third period the Broncos
  fought back.

Bob smiles as he finds he is
able to call the right plays
in his first pro game.

Soon the game was tied at 21
    to 21.
Now it was the fourth quarter.
The pressure was on.

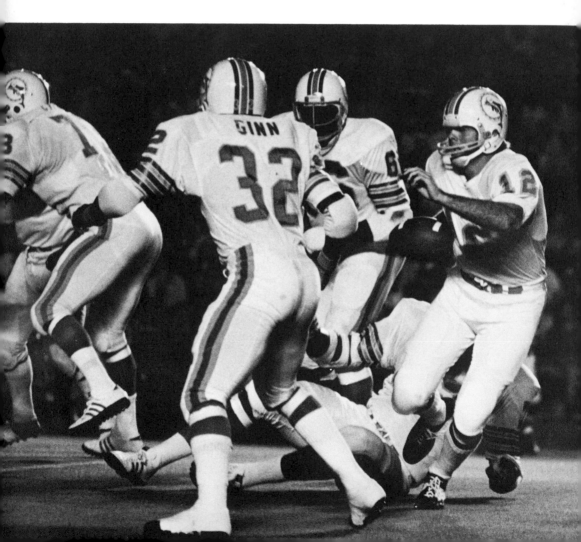

Bob Griese took charge.
He played as if he had been a
　pro for years.
He knew when to call for
　passes.
He knew when to keep the
　ball on the ground.
He led the Dolphins to two
　more touchdowns.
When the final gun went off,
　the Dolphins were ahead by
　a score of 35 to 21.
Bob Griese had won his first
　pro game!

Griese runs with the ball
like an old pro.

Coach Don Shula

4

The Big Disappointment

For three years the Miami
  team had an average record.
Nobody paid much attention to
  them.
In 1970 the Dolphins got a
  tough new coach.
His name was Don Shula.
He was determined to turn the
  Dolphins into winners.
He made the players practice
  almost all day long.

Sometimes he made them work
   out long after dark.
Some of the players hated him.
They were not used to working
   so hard.

But they all knew he was a
   good coach.
"Don't throw so many passes,"
   Coach Shula advised Bob.
"Run more plays on the
   ground."
The hard work and advice paid
   off.
When the 1971 season began,
   the Dolphins were red hot.
They won game after game.
Bob had his finest year.
His teammates admired him
   because he always seemed to
   call the right plays.
At night Bob looked at the
   movies of football games.

A tough coach watches
his team practice.

He wanted to learn all he
  could.
He made a careful study of his
  teammates and the players
  on other teams.
Knowing what moves other
  players would make helped
  Bob to decide which play to
  call.
"He always knows which way
  I am going," said one player.
"It's as though he looks right
  into my head."
The Dolphins won the title in
  their division.
For the first time they were in
  the play-offs.

Bob has a happy time in the dressing
room after leading the Dolphins
to victory in their division.

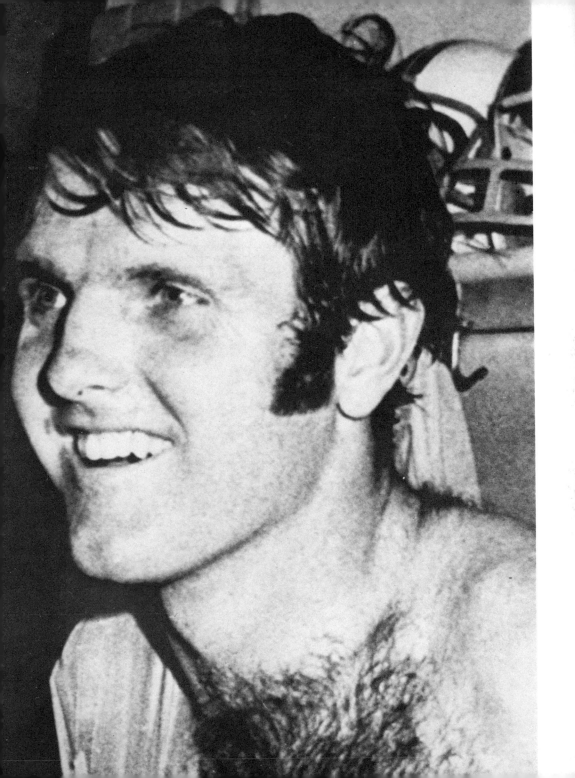

They had to face the powerful
Kansas City Chiefs.
The huge football players
rammed into each other all
afternoon.
The teams were well matched.
The game ended in a tie.
It went into overtime.
The players were very tired,
but they battled for every
inch.
Neither team wanted to lose
now.
The overtime period ended
with the score still tied.
The second overtime period
began.

A very tired Bob Griese takes
a rest during the longest game
in football history.

The game was now the longest
   one in the history of football.
The Dolphin runners were
   worn out.

Bob Griese took to the air.
But once he called a running
    play.
The Chiefs did not expect it.

The Dolphins got close enough
to kick a field goal to win the
game.
Miami won by a score of 27 to
24.
The brave young team fought
all the way to the Super
Bowl, where they lost the
championship to the Dallas
Cowboys.
The loss was a great
disappointment to the
whole Dolphin team.
They didn't want it to happen
again.

Griese fools the Chiefs
by calling a running play.

5

World Champions

The next year the Dolphins did
  not lose a single game.
They were the first pro team
  in 24 years to have an
  undefeated season.
They won fourteen regular
  games and two play-off
  games.
They beat the Washington
  Redskins in the Super Bowl.
They were World Champions.

49

Bob scores a touchdown.

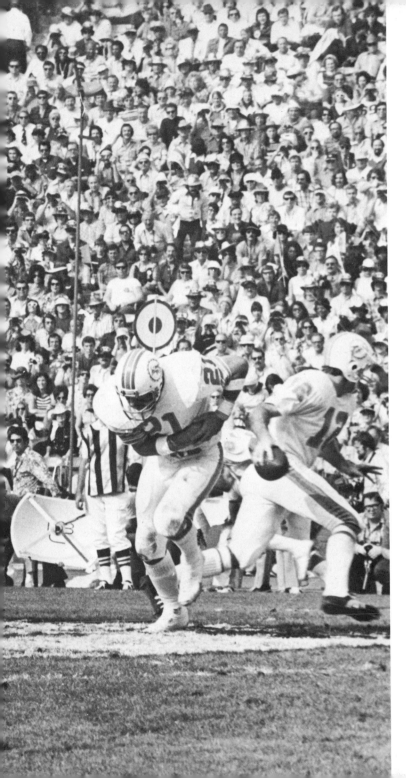

Action during the 1973 Super Bowl—the Miami Dolphins against the Washington Redskins. Dolphin teammate Jim Kiick (No. 21) pretends to be carrying the ball while Bob Griese (No. 12) runs back to pass.

Bob Griese was now a super
   star.
But it has not changed him.
Bob does not brag about how
   good he is.
He is quiet and calm.
He studies football games.
He works hard at his job, and it
   shows.
His coach and his teammates
   like him.
He is the team leader.
The Dolphins kept on winning
   in the 1973 season.
For the third year in a row
   they ended the season play-
   ing in the Super Bowl.

Bob Griese and Coach Shula trot onto
the field before the 1974 Super Bowl
game against the Minnesota Vikings.

This time they faced the
  Minnesota Vikings.
Bob was confident as he ran
  onto the field.
The Vikings kicked off to the
  Dolphins.
Bob Griese took charge at
  once.
He marched his team 62 yards
  for the first touchdown.
The Vikings ran three plays.
They couldn't move the ball.
Once again Bob took over.
He led his team easily for 56
  yards and the second touch-
  down.

Even a star quarterback can have a bad moment.
Bob straightens out his helmet after a hard tackle
during the Super Bowl game.

Gary Yepremian kicked a field goal.

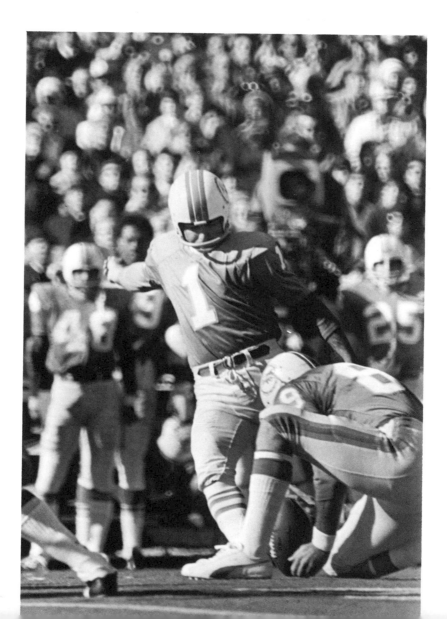

At half time the score was 17
to 0.
Bob called a nearly perfect
game.
The whole team played well.
In the third quarter he threw a
long pass.
Paul Warfield ran down the
sideline.
He made a diving fingertip
catch.
Miami was set up for another
score.
Bob gave the ball to huge fullback Larry Csonka.
Csonka ran over a few Viking
players for the touchdown.

Dolphin kicker Gary Yepremian
boots a field goal.

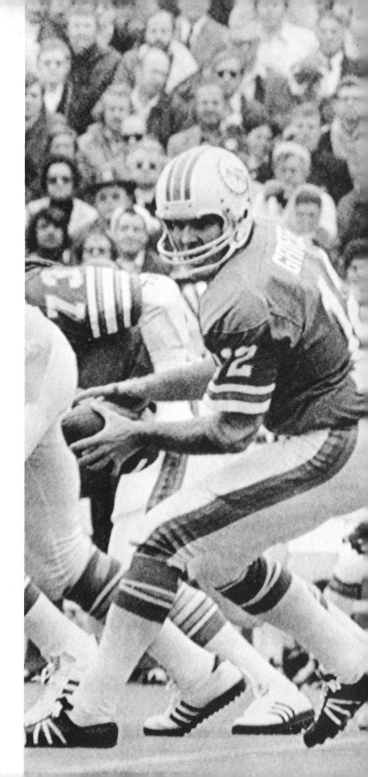

Bob Griese (No. 12)
gets ready to
hand the ball to
Larry Csonka (No. 39),
who is coming up
from behind.

The final score was 24 to 7.

For the second year in a row the Dolphins were World Champions.

It was an amazing success story.

When Bob was a rookie, the Dolphins were a struggling new team.

Many people had never even heard of the new team from the South.

In a few years the Miami Dolphin team became one of the greatest football teams of all time.

Powerful Dolphin fullback
Larry Csonka scores, carrying
Viking tacklers on his back.

It was a quiet young quarterback named Bob Griese who
led the way.

Bob Griese looks for a receiver.